✝

To M.T.

Who knew me in the Sister-Woman years and allowed me to graduate from teacher to friend. What a time it was — and is. Thanks for your friendship, and Happy Fiftieth!

          Love,
            Charlotte

20 July 2003

SISTER Woman

Poems
by
Sister
Mary
Anthony
Barr

BRITTON JAMES PUBLISHERS
P.O. Box 120907, NASHVILLE, TENNESSEE 37212

SISTER WOMAN
Copyright (c) 1989 by Sister Mary Anthony Barr
All rights Reserved

No part of this book may be used or reproduced in any manner whatsoever without permission except in the case of brief quotations embodied in critical articles or reviews. For information Address Britton James Publishers, P.O. Box 120907, Nashville, Tennessee 37212.

Grateful acknowledgement is made to the following for permission to reprint previously published material:

The Sewanee Review : "A Complaint to Her Lord in Her Loneliness," "Lament for Ritual Happiness," "To Gerard Manley Hopkins," "The Enchanted Pond: Monet at Giverny," "A New Song," "Light of Christ."

Ave Maria Press: "Enoch"

Alembic: "Letter to Paul"

America: "December Was A Different Set of Hours"

The Monacle: "Solitude in Black and White"

The Romantist: "Christopher's Song."

Photo by G.W. Austin
Art by Billy Yates
Typesetting by Sierra Copies

Library of Congress Catalog Number 89-91849
ISBN 0-9624100-0-4
Printed in the United States of America

To My Family and My Community

Many persons, past and present, deserve my thanks for personal and professional reasons. They will know who they are, and why. In naming these few, I do not exclude the others, but confine myself to thanking those directly involved in helping me publish this book of poems:

George Core
Mary Whitson Crichton
Sister Mary Bernard Curran
Jane and Walter Sullivan
Maggi Vaughn and Ron York

and, though I can thank him now only in prayer,
Allen Tate

Contents

Foreword	11
Author's Note	15
Magnificat	17
Little Hours	18
John	19
Rain	20
December Was a Different Set of Hours	21
Orestes	22
His Spokesman, Spring	23
Girls At the Prom	24
Poem for the Fortieth October	26
A Complaint to Her Lord in Her Loneliness	28
On Hearing of an Opossum... *see note*	30
To My Mother, Wintering in Florida	32
Trains	33
Lament for Ritual Happiness	34
Written in Early Spring	35
To Gerard Manley Hopkins	36
Grandfather's Glasses	37
Christopher's Song	38
Death in Autumn	40
Poem to Honor Henry Moore	42
A Song for Saint Cecilia Day	44
The Serious Discussion: Poem for Susan	46
The Enchanted Pond: Monet at Giverny	48
Enoch	49
My Star Poem	50

Adam Digged	52
Obscure Passage	53
Arbori Infelici	54
Letter to Paul	56
Nags Head Revisited	58
A New Song	59
The Binding of Isaac	60
Glory Train	62
Just So, Poetry	64
Anamnesis	65
Light of Christ	66
The Etymology of Mercy	67
Solitaire	68
Radnor Lake	69
Hurricane Watches	70
Stonehenge: The History Lesson	72
The Argument	74
Solitude in Black and White	75
Homage to Mozart	76
Bowers	80
Highlands Winter	81
Time Eating Space	82
Girl with Raspberries	84
Parable of the Ginkgo Tree	86
Starting Over, for Joanie	88
About the Author	91

FOREWORD

Dozens of accomplished poets are writing every conceivable kind of poetry in the United States—and publishing it regularly in a wide variety of forums. Never have we had so many good poets in this country; seldom have we had so relatively few great ones. In the same manner we have rarely had so little Christian poetry appearing regularly in the literary marketplace. American poetry is being written in many modes and conventions, but only rarely is any of that poetry Christian, although there is much devotional poetry of an inferior order. Whether this is a sign that we are now living in what, in certain respects, is a post-Christian age cannot be determined, but some of us may be inclined to think that. All of this is to say that contemporary poetry is battening but that religious poetry is not getting its due. We now seem to be reading Christian poetry only in a historical sense—which is to say that we are content to read it in English literature from Chaucer to Milton to Eliot and Auden but see it now chiefly as more nearly a matter confined to the past than of participating in the moving present so far as literature is concerned. Ours is a world predominantly secular.

Such a literary and cultural situation is difficult for the Christian poet who is writing traditional religious verse. This unpromising and difficult situation has faced Sister Mary Anthony Barr over the past two decades and more as she has written some of the best Christian poetry published in this country during that time. The writer does not pick his or her situation, any more than the writer can always deliberately pick subject or theme. In fact, as Robert Penn Warren and others have pointed out, the subject often picks the writer in the sense that the individual writer is doomed by background, education, mundane interests, and moral values to write about certain subjects, exploring them through appropriate themes and images. Sister Mary Anthony might well be writing Christian poetry even were she not a Dominican Sister and a teacher, for she is so profoundly committed to her religion that it seems natural, even inevitable, her poetry reflects not only this world but the world to come.

In writing "Letter to Paul," Sister Mary Anthony is presenting a poem that is Christian in argument and image but that is by no means confined to the Christian theology. "No theologies contain the God I need," her speaker says. The scene—a beach in New England—is contemporary, but the theme—the urgent need for God—is timeless. Consider another poem, "Arbori Infelici," in which a commonplace but chilling event—a boy's fall from a tree to what seems a certain death coming after a long hospitalization—brings the speaker to this realization as she ponders the fate of the boy: "Yes, inside that splintered head you know the Cross." In "Enoch," one of her most concentrated poems, Sister Mary Anthony celebrates the life of Thomas Merton by contemplating the significance of his accidental death by electrocution: "You, like the flaming monk's palm pinned up to/A desert sky, ascended through sparks into ash..." "Sweet Christ," the speaker then cries, "how terribly his beauty burns us now!" In each poem the movement is from the mundane mortal world to the timeless realm of spirit. That also applies to poems that are essentially secular in nature—such as "The Enchanted Pond: Monet at Giverny." The old artist decides that the artist acts by being an eye reflecting light. And, by the end of Monet's life and this poem about his late years, we realize, with him, that seeing is not merely a matter of the eye and that the light comes from within the artist as well as without—and that the light reflecting off a small pond can reveal the world to us. Such are some of Sister Mary Anthony's subjects—the seashore, a dying boy, a dead monk, a great artist at life's end.

A more representative poem is "A New Song," in which one fall day a wasp struggles upward "from the altar of sacrifice" in church. Seeing that lonely wasp, an insignificant but feared creature with a terrible sting, shocks the speaker into a renewed awareness of the sacramental world. There is an implied metaphor that we realize in meditating upon the wasp's painful ascent, which represents our own tortuous struggle to achieve redemption. Hence the pun when the speaker is "stung to the heart" by a sharp recognition. She recognizes what Gerard Manley Hopkins (the subject of another poem collected here) means in saying "The world is charged with the grandeur of God." Hence her painful but joyful recognition of "worship's danger and delight."

By now I hope it is plain that this poet is writing in the metaphysical vein that Christian poets from Donne, Herbert, Crashaw, to Hopkins and, more recently, Eliot and Tate, have mined brilliantly since the Renaissance. In a famous essay devoted to the metaphysical poets Eliot wrote of their "recreation of thought into feeling," saying "When a poet's mind is perfectly equipped for its work, it is constantly amalgamating disparate experience; the ordinary man's experience is chaotic, irregular, fragmentary." In Sister Mary Anthony Barr we see the mind of the poet well equipped for its work, whereas you and I, dear reader, are more likely to find our experience is chaotic and fragmentary. Such poetry as this enables us to understand ourselves and our world less imperfectly. The sense of uncommon wholeness and of analytical sanity and wit allies Sister Mary Anthony to Donne and others in the metaphysical line, but this is not to say that her poetry is merely derivative, any more than it is solely Christian in emphasis.

In one of his last essays Allen Tate wrote of Robert Frost, the great commoner of modern American poetry, as a metaphysical poet. Metaphysical poetry is not always dense and difficult, and it often has the elegant simplicity and honest directness that we associate with Frost. Sister Mary Anthony Barr's poetry is not convoluted and precious, nor is it unreasonably difficult; on the other hand it does repay our closest attention, which is to say it is not only worth reading but rereading. Tate admired Sister Mary Anthony's poetry and enthusiastically introduced it to me, as I now, some fifteen years later, present it to you with admiration and delight.

So much for some ways of reading the poems that follow and of seeing them in the tradition of English poetry from the Renaissance until this moment. I have by no means exhausted the possibilities that inhere in this rich and diverse poetry; I have merely tried to limn some of the more prominent and significant aspects of a fine body of verse that has not received the attention that it deserves. Let us hope that the critics of the future will give Sister Mary Anthony Barr's splendid poetry the attention and praise it has already earned.

—George Core
Editor, Sewanee Review

AUTHOR'S NOTE

It seems to be stating the obvious to say that sisters are women. But I am aware, from hard experience, that a lot of people are surprised when they discover this truth. If my collection of poems helps to align the secular world's perceptions of us with reality, I will be pleased. Dispelling stereotypes is a salutary thing, as far as I am concerned.

However, my chief concern is the poems, not the image of the poet. Poets have something to say. And there comes a time when they want to be heard. Having paid my dues to the muse of this lonely art, I am ready for someone else to listen to my voice. When Eliot said there is no life that is not in community, I think he meant life for artists as much as for Christians. The Word made *flesh* is what feeds my art as well as my faith. He dwells *among us.* Poetry, like religion, is not just a personal expression; it is communal act. I may not know you, reader, but I write these poems for you.

I am also a sister of another kind. I grew up the only girl with two brothers. In my family, I was simply "Sister" long before I was Sister Mary Anthony. In fact, it was with my brother, David, when we were both in high school, that I first began to write poetry. We started together and we are still each other's best critics. Maybe the next book will be ours..."Sister-Brother." We'll see.

MAGNIFICAT

My soul magnifies the Lord;
and my body sings.
You will excuse the earliness,
caroling before Christmas;
audacious for a body
that's a child's,
unkissed and flat.
But I am the November nest,
in a brief blue season,
the seed in the snow.
God is still a mountain, yes,
a curious and high cloud.
But a wedding
with unspeakable groanings,
and a growing
in my pale abdomen,
will get us something
reaching for our breast:
Dove unfolding
in the crevice of our chest.
Blessed is the little nest.

LITTLE HOURS

The white bird
flies delicately away;
the young sun
hesitates to break
on the slender stalls;
small-voiced spouses
fill blondwood stalls,
as bedwarm hands
give Prime away.

Twenty-one bells
give pieces of day,
hour to hour,
as birds build
gradual mansions of string.
Small black words
make bread without leaven,
and the white bird's prayer
flies delicately away.

JOHN

Beloved one,
more than a young girl's
was the surge
of your white love
for the young Messiah.
When virgins embrace,
the union is not flesh,
it is fire;
and the seed endures.

All the fierce young eagles
remember a time
when friends
could be lovers;
when Mass was unsaid
and the Word unwritten,
and Jesus sat
holding the giddy head.

RAIN

The rain did not stop all that day.
It ran on the trees
and made the leaves slick
and separate;
gutter-drops filled
the cups we made of our hands,
dry things,
that water could so intoxicate!
The child came to the window
to look at trees,
(saw how sodden and soft
was the hard mosaic of bark).
The poet embraced his rug-fast tortured knees,
laid his long look and his head down,
dark at the wet window's heart to hear
the prose of earth
and his own breath loose on the glass.
He asked if the rains were Jesus' tears;
overall-vested,
he celebrated some brave inconsolate mass.
When he rose to play,
there were scratches left by his hair;
and the stain of his lashes
was on the window and air.

DECEMBER WAS A DIFFERENT SET OF HOURS

December was a different set of hours,
a once only but an always,
altogether ours.
We were christmas children,
a migratory tribe that came and went.
We moved under stars and watched our breath
spell songs upon the air.
We tumbled through the town
zippered together.
Our mittened feet held mountains upside-down;
our galoshes fingers crossed the sea dry-shod.
We were a band of believers,
loving the dead month more than any flowers.
Snow spoke back when spoken to;
angels' wings were first among all truest things,
and reindeer flew.
In our white world snowplows were the only sin.
We were as tall as holly,
we were as small and green.
Christmas children stay too high too long
to stand awake (we missed the midnight mass).
But God was born in the morning this we knew:
Kind parents woke us to say this much was true.
We were not meant to last.
In whatever workshop at whichever pole,
they made our hearts of baubles
and our souls of glass.
We were a breed the blight got to at last,
a short december weed.
It understood the universe and died.

ORESTES

They say that you have fallen out of grace
And furies follow you at head and heel;
News comes on wind, but this alone I feel:
Your face, your face is like my father's face;
And in the dust of toyland I can trace
The hobby-horse's groove and carriage wheel,
The path our childhood took from grace and weal;
And where our gods are buried show the place.
The demons of a new faith push you on,
But you renew your face upon your son;
And ride cock horses back to Banbury Cross.
Though time is not a friend, yet blood is bond:
Get daughters. Hazard wasted seed for one.
Your son will gain a lover for your loss.

HIS SPOKESMAN, SPRING

His spokesman, spring,
Says that he lives;
Says that the earth
Which had nothing
Gives lard to the bone
And leaf to the beech,
Juice to the cavity
Barren of young;
Salt to the snow
Tossed, sends rivers
Of slush to the sea;
And salt, as he saith,
Entangles the earth.

His spokesman, spring,
Says that he slumbered
On pillows of storm;
That he wakened to
Darkness and his eyes
Brought the morn.
He went forth as a
Nightling, gathered in
Gloom. He comes with
The dawn cock; now
Death is no doom.
Spring is his spokesman;
Spring says that he lives.

GIRLS AT THE PROM

NO SMOKING PLEASE
Our walls are made of lace;
Enter with imagination this place.
The best is not to grow.
Having marked the withering of flowers,
We shall save this hour annd the rose
And our young men from morning, blights,
Or wars. While we hold this pose,
Nothing wakes or fades or goes.
All who join this sisterhood must know
The allegiance we owe is to Camelot and
Spain; to castles made of air and
Arthur's brief career.
Those dragons of desire which bring us
Most pain are the last things we
Have slain. For this, and yet one further
Season, we shall string the moon and battle
Reason.
NO SMOKING PLEASE
Our walls are made of lace;
Enter with imagination this place.
Games are hazarads too;
Their gentle blows are deep.
But "Courage," say the girls in blue,
"Let us do the rites of spring before the
Unbelieving and the old."

Do not pity them.
Though death be all the fashion now and
Sappho's girls are dying before the rose
Can bloom; though all the isles of Lesbos
Lament the brides of June,
Pity not the silver girls.
They are given, like owls,
All wisdom in a night.

It was right
To teach the daughters of despair
To try the crystal shoe.
There are tasks
Beyond keeping the embers bright.
The Greeks, of course, were lying
When they recorded man.
But glorious, nonetheless, was his
Dying, and their happy celebration
Of his doom. All the classic children
Must lose the race with time. And these
Revels now are ended, where beneath a
Paper dome, the boys are hailing pumpkins
To bear the changed girls home.

POEM FOR THE FORTIETH OCTOBER

This is the fairest October (meaning both lovely and honest);
More right than the rest, though they, vintaged early,
Were sweet. But heartfood we, caring now, know is best when
Ripe, when the green is gone over and blessed by the exorcist,
Age. Let all bygones be dragons at rest.

Pilgrims who sternly come on in the damp morning light
Address us more clearly than gypsies who danced, though
There was delight in the unwilled recesses of dreams.

Gracious Libra balances waking with dreams, and holds in
Her silver twin trays the spent with the saved; holds what
You dreaded and longed for: the last of your longings,
Settling of fears, no troubled attachments of mind.

Let us welcome with (a little) wine the blood-thinning years.

O Daughter of Time, in the twin trays are body and mind.
Thou, equipoised, centered on stars and stones, midway art
Of this and that home. What tips the known in thy measure
Toward the divine?

While the indifferent clock of the world turns round,
Let us cheer that hour, the sphere of your birth, the
Fusion of ancient devotions (emotion is bitter alone.)

You were birthed in the undertaking of unalterable word;
You were uttered of duty, which is ever more fervent than
Whim. You were begotten of the Faithful in the indifferent
Face of the World.

I praise one in whom Reason was rose, was blood, was redder
Than riot; you who were never convinced, though wild
Cavaliers sang hard at the windows of Spring that we were
Not mortal, that Love was not in its way a reason for tears.

I will sing your unshakable stock, whence Christianity came,
With Dark Age survivors out of the sea and onto the islands
Of stone. You were bred of the Celtic loam wherein are tended
Together the careful Oak and the Heather that has no care but
To lie with the earth and love with its purple hands.

I kiss more in homage than passion your wrist that goes taut
Against season and stress, but aches nonetheless with the
Moon and her tides. I see that both swim in your eyes, the
Blood which has never seen air, and the airy sky.

Though druids no longer preside over forest and feast,
I do not for this time distinguish singer from priest.
The tribal repast is our Thursday pasch, is this token,
This toast; all relics, this bone.

I will lay as long as I can this green on the heart's pagan
Core for you: my scop-song, this prayer. After clergy-comfort,
The poet's song is the last. Let the poetess allay, with
Formulae old as the world, your passage in pain.

Memento mori. The leaves blow stricken, but bright.

Though gardens and moments and presence of others were deadly,
We thought them kind. May we be forgiven: we cherish our
Kind, walk slowly from what we have known. May Michael
Archangel scatter these demons (bright demons) of night; mature
Angel light put our monsters to flight.

May we recover our parents and brothers, though the leaves blow
Abroad forever; find in the night's descending our clean Irish
Homes. The Good God bless these bones, make graces out of
These shadows, whence cometh life out of the groin.

A COMPLAINT TO HER LORD IN HER LONELINESS

There is a rosebud on your altar
Which waits unopened.
Who knows if it is red or white?

I am standing at your door,
Stopping late.
I would implore that you
Search me,
That you know me,
That you open each petal.
Push my petals back.
Crush all my store of honey.
Know me at the source.
Suck the pores that sweat
Sweetness,
Sup the wine that pours.

> My hearth grows cold.
> Warm my stony thighs.
> Poke the dying embers
> Of my soul.

I cherish no long life,
Since each such act,
They say, diminishes
The length of life a day.
I would know one death.

I have bragged before the maidens,
O my Conquistador! And beckoned
You from shore, "Come farther
In this country than before.
There are mountains more."

I am more clothed than
Wintered people in the
Coldest land; yet even as
I anticipate your hand,
I am more nude than
Any woman before any man.
If you will take me,
I will shimmer like the
Morning in your hands,
Drip dew enough for
All thirsty lands.
Naked I stand.

Only if you own me is it right
To lie uncherished on my bed
Of stone.
If you are not my Knight;
If this my single cot
Is not your Throne;
And I am not reshapen
By your skill;
Then shame is to my covered
Head in light more than
To all naked girls at night.

And the red rose is better
Than the white.

ON HEARING OF AN OPOSSUM NOT QUITE DEAD AND HER OFFSPRING NOT QUITE BORN ON THE HIGHWAY

They inform me, mournfully returning from
The road, of a fellow female's plight;
Another mammalian mother is caught in the
Act between still life and motion, in the
Old ordeal of pregnancy not brought to term.
They report that she was left alive — that
Was the worst— her young excised by the
Steel midwife, between horn and wheel, in
One more demolition of the small in an
Impact the car never feels on the rolling
Road-links to the fabulous cities of men,
Where grief is ongoing, for nothing pauses
To grieve. Another creature has been too
Slow for the age. Mediation in mid-stream
Loses for ponderous rodents, and men in
Their indecision, the safety of either shore.
So the matron of woodlands can no more
Pretend sleep. She will be long away from
The glens and the coverts. Here, where
Death is real and more red than Nature's
Tooth and Claw, her eyes are wide open under
The stars on the painted street. And here
She spills all that was nourished under her
Heart onto the thoroughfare that leads to
Our homes, but is far from her own.
Passersby to the busy kingdoms slow for a
Look; she gazes back in the headlight glare,
Turns her head sideways with idiot hurt and
Gentle surprise at their approach. At her
Side, the blind possums are still who did
Not come forth to be pouched and treed and
Taught to fake slumber. "Time to Retire,"

Yawns the rubbertirebaby, and the children all
Sleep. All ye who pass on the road, look
And know that this is the intersection of
Time, where Life touches both its ends.
Travellers, weep on the windshields you
Point toward harbor and home: for the
World that miscarries its own, for the
Troubling of time. In the human race
Toward Samarra, no time to say hello,
Goodbye, we're late, we're late, we're
Late. Life goes on; the dead we must
Leave behind. In the coverage of today's
Event, this is all: The creature lies on
The road and mercifully does not judge us.

TO MY MOTHER, WINTERING IN FLORIDA

You are come round again to an even year,
The sixtieth, in the month of the lioness;
And I am brought, a Leo in the northern parts, nearer
Thirty, and farther in time's geography from your caress.

But we can go still together—I'll wear my party dress—
To the birthdays of the past, the house you kept.
I want to be amid the clutter of your dresser; to bless
The rooms you graced, the hearth you swept.

These long seasons, I have sometimes wept
For sweet trinkets I remember on your shelves;
For sachet in the sweaters, scarves wrapped
Away in scented drawers, the work of elves.

A small lady's shoes of Spanish leather I see closeted,
Or Italian, dainty makes for my small mother's feet.
The rest of Daddy's fortune went for bread and book-fed
Heads; her vanity had sandals as a seldom treat.

Larger than her person was the heart that fed
Us faith, and hand-me-downs to kinfolk, and bequeathed
Unto her daughter woman's lore. All that I have read
Is not equal to the wisdom on that forehead wreathed.

By every wrinkle be your life increased.
May song of your sons, your husband, and my song
Rush out in salt-touched homage to your feet
As you celebrate your birthday by the sea; and may our wrong
    Be washed from your remembrance by this tribute's tide;
    May your wrinkles wink on us, your prints in sand abide.

TRAINS

The train passes here, between the
Golfcourse and our three schools.
It only carries freight. And who
Knows if the same train ever passes
Twice. The man who used to take our
Refuse to his pigs said it means snow
When the whistle's loud from several
Miles away and clear, across the fields.
When wailing from the trains comes strongly
Through the coldness on those days,
I sense a danger far away. I vaguely
Conjure dragons scourging distant hamlets,
Belching furnace breath and breathing
Threats to happiness and rest. Then it's
Reassurance to remember friendly, roundfaced
Locomotives from our bedtime books, climbing
Hills of conquered fright, grills bent in
Smiling concentration, mouthing puffs of
Exclamation: "I think I can! I think I can!"
Sometimes the passing cars revive a legend
Out of family lore: how my brother, brought
Reluctant to the station, clutched our father's
Hand and pressed his head into the other's
Sleeve. and while his eyes were buried in
Parental gabardine, the rails spit steam and
Our mother disappeared. His fear dates from
Then. He never would ride trains from college
Or the service when he came.
The train still passes here.
And when it fires the night ahead with Polyphemic
Eye, I wonder what has vanished in those moment-
Seeming years, while the others were not looking.

LAMENT FOR RITUAL HAPPINESS

I have been affrighted on the city streets
By serious goblins on the shoulders of the wise,
Who question my mirth, my gown, my undemise.
O they are grim with the dire pursuit of fun
And righteous casting out of grace.
There is a boorish blasphemy in every face;
There is a leer in look of girl and boy; and
All the Daughters of Musick are brought low.

Whatever worm bred joy seems no more to breed.
Yet let me be for marriage and the gilded ring,
Stay the canopy in whatever place it droopeth;
Be for chastity, mourn betrothed virgins in the
Mountain's mouth; weep at graves, then cancel
Tears when allotted month for weeping is consumed;
Pour ritual waters; purify the years. Go thy ways.
Leave tokens of man's joyfulness in every place.
Bear Duty to the vestibule of Death. Chant Evensong
In the lion's face. Be blithe. Give votive thanks.

Endure the sentence of Monday week to week.
And let me, in saying this, desist. For sayings are
Past sense. I pray this. I laugh and wink and realize
The cosmic dance. I affirm the sanity of Happiness
In the bleak night's eye. I rendezvous the crazy stars
And court the smiling God. This only magic can we
Trace beneath the unremarkable moon: that we encircle
Our descendants in the encircling gloom; and save them
In our hugging arms and crowing hearts from death or
Despair, or the deeper sadness of self.

WRITTEN IN EARLY SPRING

Crocus blink from purple lids their
Orange eye, and jonquils fiercely
Dance along the drives, begging their
Seducer, March, release them to their
Rightful groom, the Sun. In early
Spring I watch forsythia, slender
And sparse, inch along its bough;
And sense, when wanton onion blotches
Every yard, the unabstraction:

The substance of things hoped for.
When lean and longfaced Lent puffs,
Out of the hollows of his cheeks,
The shofar of the dawn, I, winter-
Widowed, meet him at the tomb;
Where, even as we wait, the
Crannies bloom.

TO GERARD MANLEY HOPKINS

We keep festival for your Jesuit brother, Gonzaga.
But I confer this once, this June twenty-first, the
Crown on the singer instead of the song. I keep wassail
For you, who understood, indeed who endured, such chastity
In mansex fine; and, Time's eunuch, cried to the Lord of
Rain as much as this saint wept his innocent misereres
On the breast of God.

Aloysius bore the plague-bitten poor on his back until
The poison oozed through to his helpful heart. He
Carried his name as a piece of twisted iron, his shame,
Until in his heart's heat it twisted straight. And you,
The shaper of song, saw in his fraternity the prize:
Prayer, patience, alms, vows; paid in an enormous dark
The price.

O impotent fisher-king! Your fathered-praise in Liverpool
Was stammered sermon like the blowpipe flame. The dismal
Port grew warm in that erection. The seeded lanes revived:
The Resurrection! Leave but ash? You left the world of
England all aflame. And where you shyly, soutaned, stood
In Oxford (St. Aloysius' Church that place's name), were
Sired words of the World's Wunderfaeder, in stuttered
Ejaculation.

Your fame, though you were reticent, retired, is shook
Forever where our language falls; and may not (this
Would be, by your rod, better praise) fail in Heaven's
Scrolléd halls. Perhaps that heaven is only peace, and
Poetry but sweetly tunéd song. Then we are lost souls
And your art's surpassed. But you are not undone, nor
Least in grace, if in the harsh world's heaving, in
Wind's burly and beat of endragonéd seas, the kingdom's
Won.

GRANDFATHER'S GLASSES

During the first Great War
The call for sepctacles went
Forth. And Grandfather rendered
Up, with 'ful devout corage,' his
Cherished pair; posted in haste
To Washington, his dearest ones.

The note commending this brave
Act was sealed Department of
The Navy, and signatured F.D.R.
The gist was: our deepest thanks,
But we shan't deprive you, Sir,
Of your prized pair. May you
Use them, in better days, again.
You are a patriot and a gentleman.
We return forthwith your Opera
Glasses. With kindest regards, etc.

Business was going badly in
Nineteen twenty-eight. Grandfather
Was said to be stooped of late; his
Pleasant mien sagged slightly day
By day. Wouldn't you know, in
Twenty-nine, Grandfather sank with
The Bank and Trust.

Grandfather was never a practical
Man (he sold the Coca-Cola stock
And kept the other kind). But he
Was a gentle, kindly man. And he
Had five stout and stalwart sons,
And he sadly shook his head as he
Launched them on Life's sea. For
He had bequeathed them all fine
Dreams, and impracticality.

CHRISTOPHER'S SONG

Christopher is stooping by the sea,
Digging with his toy blue spade
For Spanish gold. And every dune
His shovel strikes yields stones.
But every stone he touches turns
To gold.

Christopher is scooping from the sea
His Spanish castles. His towers shine;
Their battlements are gold. He sings
Beside the sturdy keep, constructed
Quickly while the tide declined.
His song is sadder with the wave's increase.
He learns at seven that his works dissolve.

We walk with him beside this southern strand;
And fear for him when he shall be a man.
When he is fourteen, shall his singing cease?
When he is one and twenty, oh what then?
Reaching for his dimpled copper hand, we grasp
Our single issue, by no one reassured that he
Will be more numerous than the sand.

Christopher is small beside the sea,
Playing with blond abundant energy beside the
Monster water waiting for the careless and the
Free. He strides complacently, trusting us
To keep such harms away. His disneyworld is
Daylight-spawned, serene and tame. Its worst
Inhabitants are woozles, and popguns are
Sufficient for that game.

Christopher is singing by the sea,
The gardener of Eden with his toy blue spade.
O Christopher, eat bitter eels and swing on
Spanish moss with all your weight and duel
The Portugese stinger, if you must.
But do not scale the grey sea wall to follow
Birds of Paradise, nor suck sweet nectars from
The Atlantean tree.

DEATH IN AUTUMN

In Memoriam, N.T.B.
October, 1974

This bus ride from Nashville to my home acquaints
Me—the third time that I take it since death brought
Me, stern-eyed, by no tears shaken, home—with the
Dry corn and a few hogs shuffling through the brown
Grass. Their bellies, swelled by summer gorging,
Scrape thistles as they pass. Denuding goldenrod,
They swagger through the dying fields in slow
Procession. They can brood and root until the frost,
And still be well; they will catch their doom the
Day the almanacs foretell.

Before Monteagle, while the heights are yet but
Hills, I am shown Maples, gorgeous and alone.
And under one a shaded bull flicks off the sun
That has his heyday in these rainless fields;
He sheds his last abundance on the shimmering barns,
On pumps that ease the lust of reddened throats, on
Fall herds basking in this dreamy dell which soon
Will wake to market, stung awake to trucks that
Trundle cattle, by the farmer's knell.

Passing Sewanee where he studied, who now is smug
In vaster knowledge, I lean to glimpse the sandstone
Halls of learning fom my Greyhound, a conveyance
Much unequal to the train called "Mountaingoat" which
Bore my father hence in days gone by. I gaze at this
Brave bastion of our Southern past, whose gentlemen
Are indifferent to a gentleman's decease; and then
Descend, in company with covites eastward bound.

Tiftonia then; and beyond the river's bend, Point
Lookout guards the valley. At its foot the man we
Mourn is laid. Confederate cannon loom above him.
Could these mouths, stopped by Time, report, they
Would not boom his praise; for his grandsire was,
Alas, a Union man. Acorns that fall about his grave
Are large this year; the winter will be hard. Those
Good old folk of Chattanooga, persevering protestants,
The pride of Forest Hills, surround him.

A few fond prep school friends have taken note that
They are one old Baylor boy the less. We told them
He was dressed in red and grey; the day of his death
Was an anniversary day. We had not thought his death
Would be so mild. But we are pleased to say he dropped
As easily as these leaves are dropping in eastern
Tennessee's sweet season, fall. After such a striving
As this life was, its last expense was small.

POEM TO HONOR HENRY MOORE

I would carve, if chisel fit as well as pen
The clench my hand makes for the work of
Praise, a monument to him who bored a hole
In the ice of this age.

I would fit for Henry Moore a slag-heap
mountain into place, that says monumentality
Has place against our petty skies, if only
To accuse our stunted race.

I would, if I could see him in the face,
Say: "Yorkshireman, you honor us beyond
Our frail deserving. You lay embarrassing
Bigness on us. We are frightened by your
Forms. Serene in stone, your shapes recline
Along the shingles of our dreary shore.
Washed with peace, they trouble our
Proceedings. They are round. They give our
Grasp no hold. They loom outside the margins
Of our greed. The dust of your lusty hammer
Is a pollen shaken. Moorwinds carry it.
The hills break forth with bloom."

I would etch in stone a thousand-storied
Tribute, were I scion, as he is, of the
Tuscan Titan, to this gaunt great British
Man: his blesséd hands.

Thank him that there are no surprises,
Only certainties in all he ever wrought.
Weep that he is old. Then turn you to a
Sharper land, and cold.

But glory, earthlings, that in his work-
Shop still, before it rests, his hammer
Beats you out, majestic; metes to you the
Crest of all embrace:

A Moore-child clutching at your mother-
Face. Before the welders and fitters
Replace him, praise him: who magnified
Before the Lord the human race.

A SONG FOR SAINT CECILIA DAY

        I have no music.
        I have these words
    that want to be bestowed
    and have no avenues but sound.
With some hard working and good hap,
Words can come to music. Meanwhile,
My head goes laden with sweet freight
        of syllable and stress.
        I bear these words.

Times I tried to turn, to ply and hone
        these words
To Saint Cecilia's praise were luckless
Till I saw and heard one play and be as
Saint Cecilia might have been and played.

        I say that she
    was innocent and glad and
    rich in Heaven's better beauty,
        Grace.
    She sang her song
        for the King.

As His elder daughter, Wisdom,
Had touched Creation's keys in Life's
Bright dawn, just so has she (though
one might say the mode
is minor key); for truly,
Through her fingers runs God's glory;
        She has no stops
        of self to hold it in.

              And I who had no music:
    The key to my soul's close-locked tune
              is turned: My song is found.
                Whereas I stood
              hungry-eared, in faded wedding
              garment, sheltering the oil-
              spent lamp, I am swayed to
              music, borne on sound, restored
                to my first love.

And now Cecilia, I can sing to you:
O I have waited long to tell you this:
Immortal by your artless death,
You suffer mortal art to come to you.
You are the Church's neck;
You bear her song. Nero's lusty lyre
Nor Nero's fire could quench the canticle,
              the crimson praise.
              Cecilia, holy virgin,
These hands that play unaided no right notes
Recover harmony in prayer to you.

THE SERIOUS DISCUSSION: POEM FOR SUSAN

She came back to say whatever it was that she
would have been sorry had been left unsaid if
she had died that night, or if I had; because
she had heard of a friend whose friend had died
in her arms in one of those sudden senseless
fatalities with cars.

So runs the world away, I thought, as I stood
where she had hailed me in the rain and stared
at this woman-child, whom death had turned out
of the learner's desk in my classroom and scared
such sense into that she might now sit with sages.

Nodding as though I understood and could control
with my professor's head the untaught thing she
feared, I listened as my student spoke of death,
my own heart beating with her fears and bending
with its pain my two arms to embrace her in the
rain, to hold her questioning face between my
answering hands and say with the assurance that
April gives the earth, "My dear, no death shall
ever touch you."

When we parted, I watched her cross the soggy
yard, her bluejeans clinging to her wet and
healthy skin; and I could not distinguish then
the rainfall from the tears that filled the eyes
that watched her go.

She drove off in her mother's car, brought because
the tires were safer than her own in rainy weather.
But any car, I told myself, could send her reeling
on the slick black street to death. As she crossed
the bridge over our innocent creek, I longed to run
ahead and rout the trolls that might be sulking in
the caverns underneath.

But I am kept from foolish things like that by a
realism bred into the Christian bone, and in this
case, by another of her stories who would have been
the object of my chivalric mission to console.
Assigned in class, it was a recollection of her
father's death, which had not hurt, she said, so
much as her neighbor's lie that everything would
be all right and he'd not die. To never tell her
that had been my lesson from the essay I assigned;
for I am not so old that what my students teach I
cannot learn.

Death's a serious discussion. So is love.
My grade that night was earned.

THE ENCHANTED POND: MONET AT GIVERNY

"Those are pearls that were his eyes."
—The Tempest

Old monomaniac Monet from cliff walks
Turned cataract-encrusted eyes aside to gardens,
Reduced the whole horizon to a sink of waterlilies
In a cultured lawn.

We do not know what these things are that haunt us.
The Sistine painter lying prone squinted up and
Said, "This thing means that...Back of this
Lies that."

The old modern hunched a score of years above the
Lily spawn and said, "The eye does not perceive the
Thing, but only light reflecting light.
The artist is the eye."

Of times past, of times to come, there is not left a
Stone upon a stone. The Goddess of Reason was
Buried at Giverny. The waters of impermanence
Flow over her.

Claude Monet at eighty wrought this wonder with a
Trembling hand. For a moment the scales before
His eyes dissolved, and all the problems of
Light were solved.

Then he paddled off across the magic pond,
With this instruction, "Bury my body in a buoy."
So much did he trust surface, so much despise
The deeps.

ENOCH

In Memory of Thomas Merton
"Look how fast I dress myself in fire!"

The dark lightning felt your breast like a lover.
And the bells, contrary to legend, summoned thunder.
The Christ of the burnt men seared your heart with
His hand, signed you with His sign: *cruz, croaz, crux;*
And you, like the flaming monk's palm pinned up to
A desert sky, ascended through sparks into ash;
And thence into glory: the *epektesis,* at last.
Sweet Christ, how terribly his beauty burns us now!

One sermon more, and there is no more story.
So you disappear.
And the bells, as you predicted, like bridegrooms
Embrace you, filling the echoing dark with
Love and fear.

They have planted you under a cedar tree.
They will think it in future the bodhi tree.
Meanwhile, in realms beyond thought, our
Mentor sits perched (and grinning like a
Gargoyle on the belfry) in his snug Fire
Tower, guarding the abbey and hills;
His, the whole forest of trees.

MY STAR POEM

Dante clambered to the rim of hell
Scaled purgation's peak
And was caught up to paradise.
Three times he came to the limit
Of language and of space
And every time the word he spoke
Was stars.

Even since the chain of being broke,
Poets have assured us of the steadfastness
Of stars.
If not much else eludes old chaos and
New myths, at least, if Keats and Frost
Can be believed, stars do.

And now *Time* says on good authority
That stars are time-locked too,
Cycled with the rest of us to birth
And death. Science has eased us
Of the weight of spaces infinite
And immortal galaxies.

But I am stubborn and find even
In this news a poetry.
For it seems that seeds of dying
Stars furrow the fields of heaven
With such life as later blooms in
Embryonic stars. The earth, our
Sun, and we ourselves are phoenix-
Risen from such starry ash.

So what reports of planetary death
Can mar the tidings that a
Child is born?
What velocities and vapors need
Be feared, when the nearest
Star has come, been here,
And we have not been burned
Or blown away, but warmed
As by a tender breath
And our tears dried
As sunlight dries the grass.

I have stood on Bethlehem's plain
And gazed, as though the vault
Of heaven were my floor, through
A Golden Star above the mound
Of earth where God came down.
At the place of the Avatar,
I have knelt to Christos
In His cords of flesh.

What are facts beside my evidence?
I have a friend whose very eyes
Are stars; whose friendling is a
Constant Christmastide.
By such lights I have kept
On course, though spun about.
I am on this journey.
I have come this far.
Astronomy has too much to know,
Astrology too much to guess.
About the heavens I am merely
Sure of this:
There are regions I shall go
When passage is provided
Through this darkened glass.
I am on this journey.
I shall sail home by stars.

ADAM DIGGED

The father mentioned that his eldest,
That brilliant boy, our scholar,
Hired his scrawny arms and heavy
Brow for two an hour, digging graves.
No market there for charms, or faint
Alarms about the eschaton. Our exegete
Will find no clever lines in the fifth
Act opener for the learned sons of
Deposed kings to speak, while cockney
Heroes mine the wisdom of the bedrock
Ground and heave old jesters' skulls
Out of ignominy for the fetid crown.

Pardon the piling up of metaphors,
But this is the sequel to the parable:
In the unpublished portion (whispered
To the apostles when the crowd had left
Which only understood the fatted calf),
The prodigal doesn't stay. Though
Fathers are lavish, the best is thrown
Away, Kiss them and ring them and
Shoe their feet: you will not keep
The sons from the swine; or gravemen
From their task, alas.

OBSCURE PASSAGE

I think that naked boy in Mark must have been
Your rich young man. (We assume the poor slept
In their clothes). Not that it matters and
Even the venturesome exegetes leave him alone.
Except I like to think that just for once,
He did leave everything because of you.
Maybe after that wild night he returned,
Staring into the afternoon, where other
Nakedness than his was on display, where
You might turn on him, oh might, another
Look of love.
Or maybe he came later on the scene:
The garden, there before the women,
So early he could see the feet he couldn't
Follow flutter free in flight;
Stretching his glittering fingers to arrest
Another useless linen in its fall.

ARBORI INFELICI

Didn't I tell you time and again,
Be careful where you play, boy?
And though the schoolyard was treeless,
Didn't your folks say it plenty at home?
But no matter, that was yesterday and rue
Won't wake you from the days on end sleep
That engages all your fierce attention now.

Do your brothers and sisters gape at you
Amid the tubes, the ticking monitors?
Maybe they've a mind to sing to you
(Marveling that you stay abed so long)
Wake up, wake up, you sleepy head!
The wonder for them is not that you cling so
   wondrously to life,
But your unaccustomed quiet.

The scream, the slivering branch, the silence after.
Perhaps they stop, respectfully, at their play,
And stay a moment where you fell, staring accusingly
At tree and ground; or scan the sky for reasons,
Curious like you, only finding the unexplored to be
Depths now, not heights: regions where their
Brother's laughter spilled and disappeared,
The brain's dark canyons where he wanders out of reach.

And we adults: what we didn't tell you doesn't matter;
What we said became your ladder, rungs of repetition:
My son, hearken to my instruction, let your reach
Exceed your grasp, don't be satisfied, keep straining,
   never stop.

When I saw you last, you were breathless, beaming
By my side, your final report card in your grimy hand,
Thanking me for turning D to A with my magic pen.
Oh, I didn't give you that; you earned it.
You were a climber weren't you, charming Billy?
I'm not surprised you picked the inaccessible tree,
Just dismayed I didn't foresee and couldn't forestall
The hard descent.

I commemorate you on the Exaltation of the Cross,
The feast in my belief falls not without purpose
Near your fall (sparrows count for something, boys
    far more).
The sentence passed by Pilate in a different case:
Arbori infelici suspendito, puts your case in mind,
And your unlucky tree.
Should we likewise call your killer the Sweet Wood,
And sing the *Dulce Lignum* for your rites?
Yes, inside that splintered head you know the Cross.
And it is meet and just I sing my verse,
Flecte ramos, arbor alta.
Bend your branches, tree so high,
And lay your burden gently down.

LETTER TO PAUL

I write to you from the ocean's edge, near Narragansett,
A port more westerly than Caesar or the Barque of Christ
    could carry you.
I write with a western mind so tired of all that thought
    has brought it to.

A man waving his son out of the surf from the seawall of
    his summer place
Said the boy works his day around the tidal charts,
Which he knows as other boys know baseball scores;
No crest will take him by surprise.

But I've no wish to know the sea that way;
I want no science, but only what I see.
You could say I'm clinging to the mystery.
Just let these unexamined waves come into me and cleanse
    the clamor of the things I read.
The book unopened on my lap is *Prayer in Paul;*
But it is no prayer.
No theologies contain the God I need.

Joined with creation's groaning I will groan, My God! My God!
My Lord is on the immensity of waters;
What care I that He wears a robe of mist?
Brave Point Judith Light is my example;
I see His night and He my faith's small light.

This is no bather's beach but strand of stones where
    stranded things have died.
We found a piece of planking, token enough to turn my mind
    to shipwreck in an ancient storm.
Once I met a Maltese priest, who said they feel for you
As if that winter with them had been yesterday;
Nearly every boy in Malta is named Paul.

I love you too, for being a survivor.
Except for once when caught to heaven and once thrown
      to earth,
You sailed in fog.
From you I've learned to dwell as though departing,
And past all christologies to cling to Christ.

NAGS HEAD REVISITED

Once horses ran along this rim of east America,
And once men flew, rattling down dunes at
Kitty Hawk (an exclamation mark on history, as
A parenthesis of sea oats offered foliate homage
To the wobbling bird) then wafting into skies to
Rob from gods and gulls the startled seas.

But always men sailed, edging the tricky shoals
Off Hatteras, blessing in their peril the steady
Light, through waters that teach the sailor's
Heart the shallows' worst is seeming deep.

Ferrying across to Ocracoke, we too were pulled
Upward, out of ourselves; brows beaded by spray,
We wanted our salt-crusted lashes to shield us
From too soon coming to land. But we were not
Able to pretend the voyage long; no use to
Gather shells we knew, or hoard immensities.

Memory soars then drops, the mind's eye swinging
Between dark and light, as once along this
Carolinian strand illicit lanterns warned off ships.
Verges recall limits aspiration must keep.

A NEW SONG

At the commingling of the elements this morning,
A wasp staggers up from the altar of sacrifice;
Drunk on wine fumes maybe, or merely old,
The remnant of a fall unseasonably cold.

A sort of russet flame dislodged from beeswax wick,
The insect ascends, reels up through sacral sanctuary air.
Skirting chrysanthemums and candlesticks, wings sick but
Shining add a touch of jet to reds and golds.

Leveling off above the ineffable *liturgia* performed below,
Our day's distraction wobbles onto a webworked corner
Of the tetrahedral windows, choosing the Divine's;
Undaunted by an eagle's prior occupation of the place.

From hooded eyes that guardian of the evangel of St. John
Gazes imperturbably at matter, in this sphere where
Bird, bull, and lion reign, removed from sense to symbol.
Neither Narnia nor *Basileia* acknowledges a hornet's sting.

But I see only this insignificant thing, enjoying
The intrusion sidewise from my chapel stall, noting
A herald worthy of the name in one assigned to punish Adam
And now blotching the symmetry of these pillars of the earth.

Turning my eye from them whose message shook the world,
And from their word refracted in the window-piercing sun,
To this one, potent, in his weakened state, to speak.
I heed his proclamation that what's earthen is the Holy's root.

Does anybody else detect the *canticum novum* entrancing me?
Do angels flanked about us shield their eyes at this,
Their alban wings atremble as I am, stung to the heart,
And wide awake this morning to worship's danger and delight?

THE BINDING OF ISAAC
(After Elie Weisel's Lecture on Job)

Elie Weisel, scholar, is also a survivor
    of crystal nights and camp fires and
    whole burnt offerings.
He knows a thing or two about sacrifice
    and the absurd demands of Israel's
    God, how Yahweh mocks himself seemingly;
Bestows, revokes, gives again, gratuitously;
Hebrews say it is "the binding of Isaac"—
    their history, the mystery of election,
    in other words, the hell of being chosen.

Isaac, whose name means "Laughter",
    almost died beneath his father's hand;
Elie Weisel's father died just hours
    before the liberation; words and hugs
    of his son notwithstanding, he despaired.
Abraham's "road out into Godforsakenness"
    led him to faith; at the journey's end,
    he saw one son become a galaxy, a grain
    of sand the bed of all the seas, one seed
    a billion golden sheaves.

Isaac's vision was none of that, but flash
    of silver and the sky pulled back: what
    no man can see and live; no wonder when
    he was old he could not tell his sons
    apart, but had to touch the one his tongue
    should bless.

Isaac died, the speaker said, "saturated
    with days."
In all of scripture, the lecturer explained,
    only twice
    this phrase:

Once at the end of Job
And here when Isaac,
    blind from looking
    at God's flashing blade,
    went to join his father,
    where the bound are loosed
    and laughter sounds the same
as tears among the indiscriminate shades.

About himself our speaker was discreet.
"Suffering," he said, "bestows no privilege."
Elie Weisel believes, now, only in the text,
    the page,
    *Torah;*or
    more than the Word,
    the mind that worries
    with the word,
    the talmudic teasing
    argument with God.
His mind, taut as a bow, is beautiful;
His fingers know the page as lovers know the body;
He shows the *goyim* how his kind have conquered woe and rage.

GLORY TRAIN

For the Barber Family

"Grandfather has gone to glory," the grownup said.
What was glory, the grandson wondered; and rolled
The word around inside his childworld, where it
Bumped against collected mysteries: other words he
Didn't know but liked, such as "cherubim" and "mauve"
And now this word, "glory"; places, too, some that
Frightened him: "funeral home" where Granddad had gone,
Where they were taking him, where "Death" whom he also
Didn't know was waiting, or whatever people do who
Aren't alive.

Life he knew. And the moments of intersection between
Two lives, his grandfather's and his own. What they
Two had done together he understood and knew he ought
To store away with items of importance, things to be
Remembered.

He kept one actual and one mental treasure box. Inside
The actual one in the corner of his room were toys he
Never gave away and rarely lost: among them this train
Whose locomotive he had decided now to give to his
Granddad.

Gifts were part of life, the realm he relied on, a way
To reassure himself that people part from things, and
So from other people; or perhaps to say to his child-
Soul, no one goes away forever, the ones we love
Come home.

But these are reasons added by adults. The boy loved
And gave, unreasoning. Grandfather had given presents
And so would he. He did not think, tucking the engine
Under his Sunday coat, cradling it beneath his heart
That said rhythmically to his head, "Granddad's dead";
Poets and parents conjure reasons for the deed, find
Metaphors for things that children claim or render up
As things.

Only now the locomotive is a symbol for the journey,
"The undiscover'd country from whose bourn no traveller
Returns."

Then, and still in childminds, it was just a gift, a
Way to say good bye concretely. Of abstract words:
Kabod, Doxa, "the weight of Glory"; of concepts cold
And imageless, "Heaven", "Salvation", "Eternity", the
Child is ignorant. But the weight of metal in his hand,
The cold hand of his grandsire upon satin, he could feel
And understand.

Later he could know his gift bespoke more than his gesture
Meant: How God had long ago anticipated it by sending for
Someone He loved
A chariot of fire.

JUST SO, POETRY

The way water traveling down your wet arm
inevitably finds the dry page of the book
you've brought to the bath because you could
not put it down,
just so, poetry,
when we mingle the mental with the mundane,
will usually wilt under efforts to say well
what felt good, and to keep both language
and feeling from falling away.
From touching the mind to the real what's
left when the finger is lifted but stain?
O but sometimes,
as when coarse hands in the loose soil tell
the head, *"Legume,"*
and the tongue tastes the word,
rootword, wordroot, root and word:
As close is the poet joined with the
syllable as lips cling in love or close
in thirst on the cup.
Often in bonding pure thought with thing,
there's only the blot, the stain.
But O sometimes,
the right word,
the bright seed,
the blossoming!

ANAMNESIS

Turning pages of the Apocalypse
Recalls pansies you pressed in
Bible pages summers I knew you.
I find them still between theophanies
And, more frequent now, days of *Deus
Absconditus.* Funny that pressed
Flowers from those New England Junes
Can, sapless, nonetheless stir words
In me, make almost of one alone a
Hundred forty-four thousand strong.

It makes me think that God's wild
Words are tamed by what we do, that
One iota like a friend's "Remember
Me" can awaken hearts, revive old
Wombs, and ratify this earthly tent.
Flattened by the pressure of these
Years, could I find in buds as
Brittle as Ezekiel's bones the
Watered seed, or read upon the
White stone's face *Misericordia?*

LIGHT OF CHRIST

"Others were set on fire to serve to illuminate the night when daylight failed."
—Tacitus, *Annales*

The record of taciturn historian, Tacitus, attests
Even pagan circus-goers were offended the night Nero
Threw open his grounds for the display, then posed
As a charioteer and ranged among the populace by
Human torchlight.
Even the average *vir* could see that thus to see
Was to be in darkness deeper than the wine-dark sea.

Those who shone in Christus' name on neronic revels
Beheld the height their flame could rise, the depth
Descend; peering into his broiling chest before it
Caved, curled, and rained black drops upon the fields
Of Pan, each perceived in a flash, the twinkling
Of an eye, but where no trumpet swelled, the Daystar
Rising in his heart.

But for the stench one might have thought those clouds
Mixed with the Tiber mists at dawn were pious incense
To the gods of Rome.
Hagiography would in this with history agree:
Heroes are needed by and need their neroes;
Only Gods who suffer claim their hearts.

THE ETYMOLOGY OF MERCY

Your words connect with other things I'm learning:
Your instruction that the womb is just a muscle.
You demonstrated with a cutaway model, deftly,
    with your surgeon's fingers.
Sorry, you said, you couldn't cut through
Uterine walls there and then, to show me that
    there's nothing to it.

And now, in the aftermath, I send these lines
That fill the silence of a silent clock,
These notes for my gynecologist:
How it surprised me to be delivered of a
Mass of tissue which might have sheltered
Someone from the shocks of birth until his hour,
And to find the matter far less theoretical
    than I supposed.
Let me probe this feeling for you:
I was hysterical, meaning I suffered in the womb.
True, sterility but confirms what I have chosen.
But I desire posterity as much as you.
God-fearing women account the barren one accurst
And so do I.
It were better I had never lived
Than I should not let Love grow quick in me.

As for you, physician friend, you were my Luke.
And I had no one but you when my hour came.
Under your cool white coat and cooler mien
Were springs of tender mercy (one more note:
The Hebrew word is *rahamim,* from *rehem,*
    mother's womb).
Maybe we've both learned what the mystics know,
    that God is Mother.
I know it was your hand that did His healing.
The heart, too, is a muscle.
It aches for mercy more than health.

SOLITAIRE

Picture me, shuffling your mementos,
Spreading them fanlike on the floor,
Turning them over time and time again,
Each time as though I'd never seen before
Or read the wonders, words, the trivial
Fond records.

My fingertips peruse these surfaces
As the blind their braille, for messages
Already memorized. As children, given the
Initial cue, can give the whole recital
Flawlessly, so can I, from any part of these
Heaped trinkets, recite every syllable of
The romance.

When I think your treasures there, my trove
Here, these tokens that we two amass in our
Small rooms, can summon memory and fix thought's
Stability through whirling time, I dread to think
They are but things which conjure you, and might
Conceal:

Then I pray the harder that the hungry mouth
Of Lethe won't consume such crumbs as my remembrance
Scatters in the wood between our solitudes, and am
Consoled that what one discards becomes the other's
Hand.

The wonder of love is nothing's lost but what is not
Bestowed.

I picture you, northwest of me, ringed with all that
Wealth. Will you still call it *Solitaire,* knowing
I, southeast of you, am playing too? By the second
Definition we can keep the name: *a gemstone set alone,*
As in a ring.

Yes, your gifts enfold, enfoil, they harbor me.
I send you word that I am happy; life is rich; I sing.

RADNOR LAKE

TO M.W.C.

We both love such days we said,
Wet, grey but the greyness
Gleaming like a pearl;
Our serious walking shoes were
Pairs of magnets, caking onto
Themselves the layered leaves;
Weighting the other end of our
Heavy conversation, stuck with
The force of electric ideas;
Loosened after with our laughter.

I thought of a lake more distant,
Wondering, but not asking
If you too connnected
That time near Epiphany with this;
When we posed each other in fields
Of unbelievable green, and spooked
The sheep; our cameras lost them in
The mist, where one pony, finally,
Stood still.

I wanted to ask you how
Often those as close as we connect; I
Mean (we both like Greek —
Logos is a synonym for *Arithmos* and
Both mean Relation, that is to say,
Proportion; and that is to say,
Harmony) whether you notice too
How much in sync our thoughts grow
As love grows.

The answer is I didn't have to ask;
The poem's an afterthought, as all
Poems are.
The facts are the final truth:
We walked, we talked, we found
The harmony, once in County Kerry
And one Sunday in October, here.

HURRICANE WATCHES

In this evening's news, we watch the East Coast
Bracing for Diane.
With gathering alarm, the experts warn that she
With deathly-fingered dawn may touch Wilmington.
Her mincing eye is believed to be fixed on some
Lonelier line of beach off South Carolina.
It is hoped her hungry maw may surfeit find
With sea oats.

In hurricane weather, I would tell Hopkins,
Though he only thought it, surely, in his
Novice phase: I have not gone, nor have I asked
To be where no storms come. Neither has the
Love of this world nor á Kempis's *contemptus mundi*

Availed against the green swell. Life makes its
Claims. In middle age I ask if I was well advised
To be "out of the swing of the sea"?

I turned, as the saying goes, my back upon the world

In the year that a great hurricane last hit the east.
Coming just shy of a quarter-century, that span is
Enough to make one understand what voices from out

The Whirlwind might, and might not, answer to our
Cries of pain.

I do not only hear of wars and rumors of war.
There are pleasures, and yes, I dare say joys,
In the wayfaring; works and workings-out of plots
That are more poignant than the sweetest or the
Safest ends. I would say I am content to know I
Shall not hear the voice that speaks of peace
Speak here.

In the wake of some greater storm, will some poet
Of the latter days celebrate in an unimagined
Technocratic tongue our ruins? Sing to the lay
Of his electric harp, "The wielders and wrights,
Where are they?"

Well-wrought this wall; such a handsome seawall!
Came the day in mid-September, nonetheless,
Wyrd broke it.

Tell the summer people sipping nervously their
Tonics, "Alas, bright cup!" It little matters
That they reinforce their walls. Let them weigh
This in their wit: "Storms break, then wanness
Cometh."

Against God,
Whether He uses time or tides
To bear His speech, there are
No braces.

STONEHENGE: THE HISTORY LESSON

Wiltshire, 10 January 1984

Whether as sightseers, travellers, or pilgrims to a shrine,
I am unsure; but come we did, nearer to Twelfth Night than
    the summer solstice, to the Plain of Salisbury.
We came to see what things are what in the wide world, what
    events there are in the womb of time to be delivered.

Stonehenge is that place of doors which are destiny but not
    a destination; they lead noplace except to where
"The whirligig of time brings in his revenges."

Thus was I led to my own, and the others to their thoughts:
How the priories and abbeys of olde Engelond were withered
    all by the breath of monarchs who turned out to be not
    ague-proof, was my preoccupation;
And who the brazen friar was who riled the Devil so to
    bruise his discalced heel; and was the hellish stone
    indigenous to Earth?

These sarsen stones from Marlborough Downs and blue stones
    from Prescelly Hills in Wales were old when Lear was young.
Marks of some devotion older than the Druids, they marked the
    Avon's course before there was a town to house John
    Shakespeare's son.
Tom Hardy's Wessex was unimagined in the brain of an unborn
    Dorset boy when yeomen farmers, in their feudal practicality,
    mined their medieval homes from Bronze Age fields.

Since processions formed along the Avenue for sacrifices on the
    Altar Stone, Tess and her Angel Clare have chanced upon "A
    very Temple of the Winds"; and since Tess slept there,
Olivier has laid his brave Cordelia where, as she has no breath
    to stain the stone, the rack of life will not stretch her out
    again.

For the historian everything connects. So where's the lesson
Stonehenge provides from its long view of things?
What did the storm teach Lear that his old age had not?
Is Life a wheel that goes somewhere, or simply the turning
> Wheel that stays as backdrop to our mad scenes on this great
> Stage of Fools?

The details were as vital to its builders as the cubits of the
Temple were to Solomon's artisans: a double circle composing
> an outer ring with upright jambs and lintels, then an inner
> horseshoe of five pairs of trilithons.

What does it mean now? And does the meaning matter?
I say it does, and not at Midsummer sunrise only; because the
Human enterprise must be counted in, if god be God, and men
> be not ephemeral as flies.

THE ARGUMENT

While we argued, the dogs were sporting with a squealing
Squirrel around our feet, which were planted under the
Picnic table with a mutual determination not to yield to
One another an inch of ground.

Honor is a poor sauce for appetite, so there we sat: the
Ham stuck in our throat, enjoying our own articulations
Far too much to stir to save a squirrel. "Nature's way"
We said, and launched another round.

Being English teachers, we harp about the life of fiction:
How conflict is the essence of the plot. Was it art's
Detachment that made us indifferent today to Nature red in
Tooth and claw; or do animals astound

Us as they rip one another apart not one whit guiltily,
While such as we chuck our spears, retrieve them politely,
And end our arguments in tears?

SOLITUDE IN BLACK AND WHITE (AFTER CHAGALL)

The rabbi could be a monk, cowled
In meditation following his *Lectio
Divina*; he holds tenderly his scroll,
Wrapped in solitude and *tallith,* sad,
And wrapt in thought.

Smiling at the wall of man in shawl
That sits before her, sits a cow.
She ruminates, or simply rests, with
Soft eye and udder; perhaps she prays
Some bovine benediction.

Between sweet beast and pious Jew
A fiddle plays, and overhead an angel
Flies, sweet-faced too, and sad.
The clouds are dark; behind them lies
The village of three domes.

The artist has no way to tell us
Whether the violin plays gay or plaintive
Melody, nor can he say what the *hasid*
Is thinking in his solitude, whether, even,
He muses in Yiddish or Hebrew.

Chagall says, simply, "See this man, this
Cow, this instrument of sound my art leaves
Mute. See them. They are all there is."
Painters, poets and composers can but match
In their own way the holy spark.

Prophets too. Not even Moses set the bush
Aflame. Yet, in the Ukraine, as in other
Holy Places, it is known among the seers
And the saints: 'It is for man to let the
Thornbush be completely penetrated by fire.'

Unless a good man read a sign, no sign is good.

HOMAGE TO MOZART: *In Festum S. Joannes Chrysostom*
13 September 1984

Allegro (Vivace): Bavarian March

I can just imagine a beautiful SS man loving The Little Prince.
"My Dinner With Andre"

Imagine them at Auschwitz having a *kultur* night, a Mozart *notturno,*
A little night piece by the prince of harmony. Perhaps the guards
Or inmates (which is which?) prefer *Die Zauberflöte*; (a friend who
Sings one of the three old women said it's sadly funny); the flute
Hath a dying fall; a *singspiel* for the forties, or any autumn; for
This eve of Holy Cross.

Pipe us music for the Holy Rood. We shall have marches for warrior
As for saint; tunes for travelling the *autoban* or the *giest's* ascent
To Paradise from the purging fire.

Wolfgang was a weaver and he made a carpet with his magic hands.
He was a *wunderkind,* our little man, and made our "divers passions"
Sound so well. I see him in my mind's eye, Horatio: Watch in hand, he
Follows in his fevered head a first performance of *The Magic Flute:*
"Now comes the aria of the Queen of Night."

He could not see the pathways to the stars were strewn with broken
Glass. (The German makes it sound so lovely: *Krystalnicht*). Was
It Reason maddened by Neoclassicist control? Can you imagine the
Beautiful SS man sitting in the golden wheat? Should the lion be
He who tames the fox's soul?

Hitler, after all, loved his dogs and married, at the end, his loyal
Lady friend. He might have been an artist or a priest, if Vienna
Had been kinder. Cities have been known to bury their best sons in
Potter's Field. No music mustered Mozart to his pauper's grave; the
Weather being inclement, his friends would not follow past the city
Gate, but left the hearse to proceed alone. Thus, did the little
Prince return to his home.

In old Bavaria, among the peasantry, the annual respite from their
Drab monotony was the Mozart festival of Augsburg. An old *frau*
Remembers all the tedious hours lost in dance, in old teutonic song.
The heart returns each August, where fingers light as filigree can,
Today as then, touch the keys just so, turning to rosecheek the farm
Wife's wrinkles; gone, with the wave of *Ludimagister's* baton, the
Unsung years.

Andante (Cantabile): A DREAM OF AMADEUS

Karl Barth had a dream about Mozart....Barth, in his dream,
was appointed to examine Mozart in theology. He wanted to make
the examination as favorable as possible, and in his questions
he alluded pointedly to Mozart's Masses. But Mozart did not
answer a word.
                                                    Thomas Merton.

I confess to you Herr Barth, and to you, Father Louis, that
I too dream of Mozart. In my dream of Amadeus Johann Chrysostom
He is a choir boy of Salzburg and sings the Requiem for a famed
Composer, whose name is Wolfgang, dead at thirty-five of debt and
Dreariness. Little Wolfgang sings for his older self with boy's
Voice and a man's full cry; sings the *Dies Irae. . . lacrymosa.*

With my own tears I cry to the composer that I cannot pay with
Music the debt all artists owe for his giving us the dream in
Which the divine child wakens. It is this child, Barth knew,
Who speaks in Mozart's music. Tom Merton consoled himself and
Barth for growing up theologians; the consolation being "There is
In us a Mozart who will be our salvation."

I cannot, like you, Karl Barth, play his sonatas in the morning
To ease the weight of dogma through my day. But with you I can
Know the love of God because dear Amadeus wrote his masses into
Undefined unladen lovely sound. And more than you, I can feel
My Catholic heart leap up with his, in our fellowship of sin,
When from this vale of tears ascend the *Agnus Dei qui tollis
Peccata mundi.* Then I pity you, for all your clinging to the
Word of God; for your religion of the head cannot compose the
Lamb for sinners slain.

In my dream, Apollonian angels, their curls like brimming cups
Of sunlight, hover in the air above the chancel. Jocose cherubs
Dangle, in gratuitous uselessness, while mortals chant the obsequies
For Mozart. At the intoning of *In Paradisum,* this childish *Chorus
Angelorum,* laughing in alleluias, comes down to rouse the sleeper
From his state. Wings part for him; he joins the mystic round-
Dance; then I wake.

The dancing chorus of the earth returns to God. I am there when
Grace dances, so I dance. And so I dream, and ever so, I pray,
Does Amadeus.

Finale (Allegro assai): Tutti Contenti

*The work is complete and finished in my mind. I take out of
the bag of my memory what has previously been collected in it.
. . .it rarely differs on paper from what it was in my imagination.*
W. A. Mozart.

John Keats was one who lived in pain and died before his gift.
He had further in common with you this: the art obscures the
Artist; almost disembodied, poetry rises out of him as *Parthenos*
From her Zeus.

They speak of this in you as "absolute musicality"; Keats called
It "negative capability"; biographers say it makes of such a life
A shadowy and stale commodity compared with the poetry, the music,
Which consumes what is inhabits.

Which of these diseases can define your deaths? It was the gift
Itself that grew in you like cancers, killing personality; art
Concealing even art; what chance had life then, or normalcy?

We see the subject, like the name that's writ in water, disappear.
For such works no price was payment, no reception sufficed to
Please. It was the inner need that caused conception and there
The agony. Who couples with the gods, surviving that, births easily.

I read that you, Mozart, were a luminous moment in musicality,
In whom all opposites united, all tensions reconciled.
You were yourself the symphonia.
I praise you less than a mere pianist could,
Yet as much as St. John- Golden Mouth would,
For aligning what we make with the
Mysterium Dei all art apes.

BOWERS

Some birds, whose call
And plumage are not pretty,
Build bowers to attract a mate.

They are inventive
In using our discards:
Beer caps, glass shards,
Foil that signals welcome
To the other bird.

Lacking their art,
I sit in structures
Of another's building.
My treasures glint
In winter light, but
Form no usable design.

The house of memory
Is uninhabitable, I find.
And birds in their craft
Are abler than poets
To use the stuff life
Throws them for sheltering
Themselves or, in love's
Season, the beloved.

HIGHLANDS WINTER

The Cumberlands, so cold this
Season that the dog's droppings
On decaying leaves make smoke;
We rise together from the bed
To scent of kerosene.
On the hill, the matchstick glade
Of skinny pines carpets the slope
With a brown needlework, while
The dog's urine freezes to a glaze
Against his favorite pine.

We wait for Christmas, which will be
No greener than the rest of winter,
Though, I still can trust, blest.
The birth we celebrate gives precedent,
At least, to what no one here chose
But all inherited, in being born
To poverty, having to offer doves
In place of lambs to buy the priestly
Prayers that will not change a life
Except to frame it in some larger
Cause than theirs.

My neighbor's greens froze overnight
And lie in death transparent near
My path. Life here is like this
Garden: green where nothing grows
And flattened into terraced rows,
Like these houses, mean and low,
Abutting rich-veined mountains
Crowned with snow.

TIME EATING SPACE

For Rob

At the estuary, where we followed the Esk
To Solway Firth, you spoke of Thomas Hardy
and The *Great Western*: how the poet's
Phrase, time eating space, phased out the
Romance of the remote, which died in steam.
As case in point you noted our progression,
Dining last week in Tennessee, motoring to
Cumbria today for tea.

I said, staring at marsh and mudflat where
The river journeyed to the sea,
That one also thought of Turner, more
Hopeful than Constable had been for Britain's
Gain from rail and steam.
Still, didn't you agree, his brushes could
Disclose the bruised places on the dauntless
Arm of Progress?

Your period to our mutual reflections was
The dream's inversion dreamed by Shelley's
Wife, the Victorians being right to fear
The monster they were making.

Since our conversation, I've come home and
You have gone to Skye.
My sky grown reassuringly dark by nine,
I lie until eleven when your northern sun
Will just be setting, and wonder what you
Did today to fill the unforgiving minute.
Playing the eccentric Yank and knocking
The competition at croquet, hitting one
Golfball into the bay, or fishing the
Trout streams in your tweeds and waders,
With delicate flies your wife found in
Kelso where the shop owner's moustaches
Were as fabulous as his fabled lore.

Time allows these pleasures to anglers
With fanatic hearts.
And they are greater than the lairdship
Of the castle, honor in the kirk, or a
Brave but doomed devotion to the prince
Across the waters.

We know those streams are shallow and
Life's a deeper business than any big
Two-hearted river, though sport has its cost
And travel shows how dear is all advancement.

The other hikers you recall were not so
Theoretical, more alive with ozone, and
Agile around the brackish pools; they had
Less to say and stepped in less manure.
When they slowed indulgently for us, we
Were heartened that love made them linger
In spaces indigestible to Time.

GIRL WITH RASPBERRIES

For Gwynn

They are blithely breakfasting all—
Men and maidens — yea,
Under the summer tree,
With a glimpse of the bay,
While pet fowl come to the knee.
                    Thomas Hardy

The girl, pink and tender as fruit,
Raspberries bowled in her willowy arms,
Rises, chirping from brambles, See!
Her smile is the sun and it warms
As she tells how she robbed from the bee.

We shall have them with *gâteau* at tea,
Strawberries over, now's their short season,
Served up on the lawn with double cream.
Not for the raspberry girl this sauce, our reason.
She wants unwashed the rubbery skin, her dream.

Her tongue seduced this morn in Cumbria's summer,
She is eating in haste the fruit, for didn't we know
After forty-eight hours the mildew molders the seed
And the meat; but did she know how spidermites blow
And anthracnose thrive and aphids feed?

Gwynn's girl-life is grave, is duty at home.
She cannot explain this yearning,
What is this raspberry joy
That is unlike any book, any learning,
That thought will soon cloy.

Youth is glad and grave so, confusion of tastes,
With red moments too — first blush and first blood.
To it blights come, such as assail
The raspberry's heart, and time's flood
Rinses fruit and glad faces pale.

Gathering berries along the seaward vale,
Girls in their raspberry days descend
The sunlit paths of song.
While we to our teas and gardens tend,
They harvest a pleasure higher than long.

PARABLE OF THE GINKGO TREE

FELLED 1989

"Cleave the wood and I am there."
Gospel of Thomas

"After-comers cannot guess the beauty been."
Hopkins, "Binsey Poplars"

Three things thrown together (para-bole) first broke
My heart, then teased my mind into active thought
This summer: the massacre in Tiananmen Square,
The death of Olivier, the loss of our Ginkgo Tree.

The connections are the private ones that poets
Make of public mattters; no necessary links exist.
On the proverbial scale of one to ten, only the
First event will rate two digits twenty years
From now: to '69's Moonwalk, Woodstock, Manson,
Stonewall, Chappaquiddick and the Mets, we add
Beijing.

But poets prioritize, to use the current word, oddly.
I mourn stillborn democracy as millions do, yet one
Old actor and a single tree leave vacancies more vast
Across my sky, being figures of the ambient light.

Students crushed by tanks, China's saplings all
Cut down, I cannot comprehend; as Wordsworth,
Enamored of the Revolution (two centuries ago
This month) could not see the horror dealt to
Millions until he saw the hunger-bitten girl.
So, strange to say, my hero's death, serenely
In his sleep, marks the end of all *ancien*
Regimes, those that were and also those I
Dreamed.

Harry, for his part, rides no more into the
Breach and it is doubtful that his pleas will
Save the Rose.

Texans may or may not cure the sickness of their
Treaty Oak.

Which is more relentless, progress or the status
Quo? The Chinese students carved their Lady
Liberty from styrofoam; she died with them; while
The great administrative axe fell soon after on the
Tree here at home whose ancestral roots we trace
To Chinese temple gardens.

Watching living branches with their rich green
Corduroy fanlike leaves cast in the truck amid
The dead, I found an image in the news to speak
My grief: "Huge streams of people fled in terror
Past blazing trees along Changan Avenue—the
Avenue of Eternal Peace."

Our Tulip Poplars, ubiquitous and undisturbed,
Waved mockingly as I turned away.

STARTING OVER, FOR JOANIE

In friendship's first flush
We sat drinking our tea.
Your son, having gone to sleep
At the breast, lay between us.

Intermittently, our eyes caressed
Him and our minds turned from him
To your other children, the boy
And girl lost at sea last year.

In the ebbing talk our glances
Met over the sleeper's head.
You said, your look full of grief
And hope, "Starting over..."

Then you spoke of a song your
Mother had written; you sang it.
"Jesus," it went, "Send me a life
Raft, a life raft, a life raft."

Incredible to me, you sang without
Irony; you sang with an iron faith.
And your voice singing more than
The song said you have forgiven God.

This song reminded me of another
Sung, not at the funeral (that comfort
Denied) but the memorial; and no, with
Yours bereft, my soul would not be still.

If the waves and winds still know His
Voice who ruled them while He dwelt
Below, then where was He last March
In the Bahamian storm?

No answer to my question came except
Your son asleep and safe upon his pillow,
This child of nature and of grace, this
Tenuous line thrown out, this hold on life.

ABOUT THE AUTHOR

Sister Mary Anthony, Charlotte Barr, was born in Knoxville, Tennessee, in 1942, and spent most of her childhood in Chattanooga. For a time she lived on Anna Maria Island off Florida's Gulf Coast, and spent a year with her family in Cairo, Egypt, during the late 50's.

Entering Nashville's Community of St. Cecilia in 1960, Sister Mary Anthony received the habit of the Dominican Order a year later. She professed her first vows in 1962 and made perpetual profession in 1965.

Sister Mary Anthony earned her B.A. at George Peabody College for Teachers in 1969. She holds a Master's degree in English from Memphis State University and the M.A. in Biblical Studies from Providence College, Providence, Rhode Island.

Sister Mary Anthony has taught at St. Cecilia Academy and Aquinas College in Nashville, as well as schools in Ohio, Alabama, Virginia and Louisiana. She worked for a time with the people of Appalachia in the Clearfork Valley of the Cumberland Mountains. Sister Mary Anthony is presently teaching again at St. Cecilia Academy on Nashville's Dominican Campus.

This collection of poems represents nearly thirty years of work by Sister Mary Anthony, whose poetry has appeared in *The Sewanee Review, The Romantist, Restoration, America, The Monacle,* and in the anthology *A Merton Concelebration,* published by Notre Dame University's Ave Maria Press.